MW00510159

# The BIG CookBook of Mediterranean Diet

*Easy and delicious, affordable, Mediterranean recipes that Anyone Can Cook at Home.*

**Susan Fabiano**

# Table of content

# MEDITERRANEAN BREAKFAST RECIPE

# MULTIGRAIN TOAST WITH GRILLED VEGETABLES

Serves 6

- 1/2 eggplant
- 1/2 zucchini
- 1/2 yellow squash
- 1/2 red pepper
- 1/2 yellow pepper
- 1/2 green pepper
- 1 teaspoon extra-virgin olive oil
- 6 multigrain bread slices
- 3 ounces goat cheese
- 1/4 bunch fresh marjoram Fresh-cracked black pepper, to taste

## Directions

- Slice the eggplant, zucchini, and squash in 3-inch lengths, 1/4- to 1/2-inch thick, and cut the peppers in half. Preheat a grill to medium heat. Brush the vegetables with the oil and grill all until fork-tender. Cut all the vegetables into large dice. (Vegetables can be prepared the night before; refrigerate and reheat or bring to room temperature before serving.)
- Grill the bread until lightly toasted, then remove from heat and top with vegetables. Sprinkle with cheese, chopped marjoram, and black pepper.

# Energizing Breakfast Protein Bars

Total time: 45 minutes

Prep time: 10 minutes

Cook time: 35 minutes

Yield: 6 servings

**Ingredients**

- ¼ cup pecans, chopped
- 2 tbsp. pistachios, chopped
- ¼ cup flaxseeds, ground
- 1 ¼ cup spelt flakes
- ½ cup dried cherries
- 1 pinch sea salt
- ½ cup honey
- 2 tbsp. extra virgin olive oil
- ¼ cup peanut butter, natural
- ½ tsp. vanilla extract

**Directions**

- Start by preheating your oven to 325°F, then brush your baking tray with oil.
- Line the baking tray with parchment paper all round and brush it with oil.
- Combine the pecans, pistachios, flaxseeds, spelt, cherries, and salt in a mixing bowl and set aside.
- Place a saucepan over medium heat and pour in the honey, oil, peanut butter, and vanilla extract and cook, stirring, until the mixture melts.

- Add this mixture to the bowl of dry ingredients and mix well.
- Pour the mixture into the prepared baking tray and smooth the top.
- Bake until it turns golden brown and the sides pull out from the edges of the pan.
- Transfer the baked bar from the tray and cut it into smaller sizes on a cutting board.
- After cooling, store in an airtight container lined with parchment paper.
- The bars can last up to one week.

# Fruity Nutty Muesli

Total time: 1 hour 15 minutes

Prep time 15 minutes

Cook time 1 hour

Yield: 2 servings

## Ingredients

- ⅓ cup almonds, chopped
- ¾ cup oats, toasted
- ½ cup low-fat milk
- ½ cup low-fat Greek yogurt
- ½ green apple, diced
- 2 tbsp. raw honey

## Directions

- Preheat oven to 350°F. Place the almonds on a baking sheet and bake until they turn golden brown, about 10 minutes.
- After cooling, mix with the toasted oats, milk and yogurt in a bowl and cover.
- Refrigerate this mixture for an hour until the oats are soft.
- Divide the muesli between two bowls, add the apple and drizzle the honey.

# Egg Veggie Scramble

Total time: 30 minutes

Prep time 15 minutes

Cook time 15 minutes

Yield: 2 servings

**Ingredients**

- 2 tsp. extra virgin olive oil, divided
- 1 medium orange bell pepper, diced
- ½ cup frozen corn kernels
- 1 scallion, thinly sliced
- ¼ tsp. cumin, freshly ground
- ¼ tsp. allspice, plus a pinch
- 2 eggs
- 2 egg whites
- Pinch of cinnamon
- ⅓ cup white cheddar, shredded
- 1 medium avocado, diced
- ½ cup fresh salsa
- 2 whole-wheat flour tortillas, warmed

**Directions**

- Heat a teaspoon of olive oil in a nonstick pan over medium heat.
- Add bell pepper, tossing and turning for 5 minutes until soft; add the corn, scallion, cumin, and allspice and cook for a further 3 minutes until the scallion wilts.

- Pour this out onto a plate and cover it with foil. Wipe the pan clean with a paper towel and set it aside.
- Place the eggs and egg whites in a bowl and whisk them together with 2 teaspoons of water, a pinch of allspice and a pinch of cinnamon.
- Heat the remaining olive oil in the pan over medium heat and add the egg mixture.
- Cook until the bottom sets, about 30 seconds, then stir gently.
- Continue stirring for about 2 minutes, then add the shredded cheese and vegetables that you had wrapped in foil.  Serve with avocado, salsa and the tortillas.

# EGGS IN CRUSTY ITALIAN BREAD

Using crusty Italian bread is so much better than the more familiar version with empty-calorie white bread.

Serves 6

- 6 (2-inch) slices Italian bread
- 1 teaspoon virgin olive oil
- 2 red peppers, thinly sliced
- 1/2 shallot, minced 6 eggs
- Fresh-cracked black pepper, to taste
- Kosher salt, to taste

**Directions**

- Cut out large circles from the center of the bread slices; discard the center pieces and set the hollowed-out bread slices aside. Heat half of the oil over medium heat in a sauté pan. Sauté the peppers and shallots until tender. Remove from heat and drain on paper towel; keep warm.

- Heat the remaining oil over medium-high heat in a large sauté pan. Place the bread slices in the pan. Crack 1 egg into the hollowed-out center of each bread slice. When the eggs solidify, flip them together with the bread (being careful to keep the egg in place), and cook to desired doneness.

- To serve, top with pepper-shallot mixture, and add pepper and salt.

# MEDITERRANEAN LUNCH RECIPE

# Green Shakshuka with Spinach, Chard & Feta

## Ingredients

- ⅓ cup extra-virgin olive oil
- 1 large onion, finely chopped
- 12 ounces chard, stemmed and chopped
- 12 ounces mature spinach, stemmed and chopped
- ½ cup dry white wine
- 1 small jalapeño or serrano pepper, thinly sliced
- 2 medium cloves garlic, very thinly sliced
- ¼ teaspoon kosher salt
- ¼ teaspoon ground pepper
- ½ cup low-sodium no-chicken or chicken broth
- 2 tablespoons unsalted butter
- 6 large eggs
- ½ cup crumbled feta or goat cheese

## Directions

- Heat oil in a large skillet over medium heat. Add onion and cook, stirring often, until soft and translucent but not browned, 7 to 8 minutes. Add chard and spinach, a few handfuls at a time, and cook, stirring often, until wilted, about 5 minutes. Add wine, jalapeño (or serrano), garlic, salt and pepper; cook, stirring occasionally, until the wine is absorbed and the garlic softens, 2 to 4 minutes. Add broth and butter; cook, stirring, until the butter is melted and some of the liquid is absorbed, 1 to 2 minutes.

- Crack eggs over the vegetables. Cover and cook over medium-low heat until the whites are set, 3 to 5 minutes. Remove from heat and sprinkle with cheese; cover and let stand for 2 minutes before serving.

# One-Skillet Salmon with Fennel & Sun-Dried Tomato Couscous

**Ingredients**

- 1 lemon
- 1 ¼ pounds salmon (see Tip), skinned and cut into 4 portions
- ¼ teaspoon salt
- ¼ teaspoon ground pepper
- 4 tablespoons sun-dried tomato pesto, divided
- 2 tablespoons extra-virgin olive oil, divided
- 2 medium fennel bulbs, cut into 1/2-inch wedges; fronds reserved
- 1 cup Israeli couscous, preferably whole-wheat
- 3 scallions, sliced
- 1 ½ cups low-sodium chicken broth
- ¼ cup sliced green olives
- 2 tablespoons toasted pine nuts
- 2 cloves garlic, sliced

**Directions**

- Zest lemon and reserve the zest. Cut the lemon into 8 slices. Season salmon with salt and pepper and spread 1 1/2 teaspoons pesto on each piece.
- Heat 1 tablespoon oil in a large skillet over medium-high heat. Add half the fennel; cook until brown on the bottom, 2 to 3 minutes. Transfer to a plate. Reduce heat to medium and repeat with the remaining 1 tablespoon oil and fennel.

20

Transfer to the plate. Add couscous and scallions to the pan; cook, stirring frequently, until the couscous is lightly toasted, 1 to 2 minutes. Stir in broth, olives, pine nuts, garlic, the reserved lemon zest and the remaining 2 tablespoons pesto.

- Nestle the fennel and salmon into the couscous. Top the salmon with the lemon slices. Reduce heat to medium-low, cover and cook until the salmon is cooked through and the couscous is tender, 10 to 14 minutes. Garnish with fennel fronds, if desired.

# Chicken & Spinach Skillet Pasta with Lemon & Parmesan

## Ingredients

- 8 ounces gluten-free penne pasta or whole-wheat penne pasta
- 2 tablespoons extra-virgin olive oil
- 1 pound boneless, skinless chicken breast or thighs, trimmed, if necessary, and cut into bite-size pieces
- ½ teaspoon salt
- ¼ teaspoon ground pepper
- 4 cloves garlic, minced
- ½ cup dry white wine
- Juice and zest of 1 lemon
- 10 cups chopped fresh spinach
- 4 tablespoons grated Parmesan cheese, divided

## Directions

- Cook pasta according to package directions. Drain and set aside.
- Meanwhile, heat oil in a large high-sided skillet over medium-high heat. Add chicken, salt and pepper; cook,

stirring occasionally, until just cooked through, 5 to 7 minutes. Add garlic and cook, stirring, until fragrant, about 1 minute. Stir in wine, lemon juice and zest; bring to a simmer.

- Remove from heat. Stir in spinach and the cooked pasta. Cover and let stand until the spinach is just wilted. Divide among 4 plates and top each serving with 1 tablespoon Parmesan.

# Quinoa, Avocado & Chickpea Salad over Mixed Greens

**Ingredients**

- ⅔ cup water
- ⅓ cup quinoa
- ¼ teaspoon kosher salt or other coarse salt
- 1 clove garlic, crushed and peeled
- 2 teaspoons grated lemon zest
- 3 tablespoons lemon juice
- 3 tablespoons olive oil
- ¼ teaspoon ground pepper
- 1 cup rinsed no-salt-added canned chickpeas
- 1 medium carrot, shredded (1/2 cup)
- ½ avocado, diced
- 1 (5 ounce) package prewashed mixed greens, such as spring mix or baby kale-spinach blend (8 cups packed)

**Directions**

- Bring water to a boil in a small saucepan. Stir in quinoa. Reduce heat to low, cover, and simmer until all the liquid is absorbed, about 15 minutes. Use a fork to fluff and separate the grains; let cool for 5 minutes.

- Meanwhile, sprinkle salt over garlic on a cutting board. Mash the garlic with the side of a spoon until a paste forms. Scrape into a medium bowl. Whisk in lemon zest, lemon juice, oil, and pepper. Transfer 3 Tbsp. of the dressing to a small bowl and set aside.
- Add chickpeas, carrot, and avocado to the bowl with the remaining dressing; gently toss to combine. Let stand for 5 minutes to allow flavors to blend. Add the quinoa and gently toss to coat.
- Place greens in a large bowl and toss with the reserved 3 Tbsp. dressing. Divide the greens between 2 plates and top with the quinoa mixture.

# Sheet-Pan Mediterranean Chicken, Brussels Sprouts & Gnocchi

## Ingredients

- 4 tablespoons extra-virgin olive oil, divided
- 2 tablespoons chopped fresh oregano, divided
- 2 large cloves garlic, minced, divided
- ½ teaspoon ground pepper, divided
- ¼ teaspoon salt, divided
- 1 pound Brussels sprouts, trimmed and quartered
- 1 (16 ounce) package shelf-stable gnocchi
- 1 cup sliced red onion
- 4 boneless, skinless chicken thighs, trimmed
- 1 cup halved cherry tomatoes
- 1 tablespoon red-wine vinegar

## Directions

- Preheat oven to 450 degrees F.
- Stir 2 tablespoons oil, 1 tablespoon oregano, half the garlic, 1/4 teaspoon pepper and 1/8 teaspoon salt together in a large bowl. Add Brussels sprouts, gnocchi and onion; toss to coat. Spread on a large rimmed baking sheet.
- Stir 1 tablespoon oil, the remaining 1 tablespoon oregano, the remaining garlic and the remaining 1/4 teaspoon pepper and 1/8 teaspoon salt in the large bowl. Add chicken and toss to coat. Nestle the chicken into the vegetable mixture. Roast for 10 minutes.

- Remove from the oven and add the tomatoes; stir to combine. Continue roasting until the Brussels sprouts are tender and the chicken is just cooked through, about 10 minutes more. Stir vinegar and the remaining 1 tablespoon oil into the vegetable mixture.

# Caprese Stuffed Portobello Mushrooms

## Ingredients

- 3 tablespoons extra-virgin olive oil, divided
- 1 medium clove garlic, minced
- ½ teaspoon salt, divided
- ½ teaspoon ground pepper, divided
- 4 portobello mushrooms (about 14 ounces), stems and gills removed (see Tip)
- 1 cup halved cherry tomatoes
- ½ cup fresh mozzarella pearls, drained and patted dry
- ½ cup thinly sliced fresh basil
- 2 teaspoons best-quality balsamic vinegar

## Directions

- Preheat oven to 400 degrees F.
- Combine 2 tablespoons oil, garlic, 1/4 teaspoon salt and 1/4 teaspoon pepper in a small bowl. Using a silicone brush, coat mushrooms all over with the oil mixture. Place on a large rimmed baking sheet and bake until the mushrooms are mostly soft, about 10 minutes.
- Meanwhile, stir tomatoes, mozzarella, basil and the remaining 1/4 teaspoon salt, 1/4 teaspoon pepper and 1 tablespoon oil together in a medium bowl. Once the mushrooms have softened, remove from the oven and fill with the tomato mixture. Bake until the cheese is fully melted and the tomatoes have wilted, about 12 to 15

minutes more. Drizzle each mushroom with 1/2 teaspoon
vinegar and serve.

# Sweet & Spicy Roasted Salmon with Wild Rice Pilaf

## Ingredients

- 5 skinless salmon fillets, fresh or frozen (1 1/4 lbs.)
- 2 tablespoons balsamic vinegar
- 1 tablespoon honey
- ¼ teaspoon salt
- ⅛ teaspoon ground pepper
- 1 cup chopped red and/or yellow bell pepper
- ½ to 1 small jalapeño pepper, seeded and finely chopped
- 2 scallions (green parts only), thinly sliced
- ¼ cup chopped fresh Italian parsley
- 2 2/3 cups Wild Rice Pilaf

## Directions

- Thaw salmon, if frozen. Preheat oven to 425 degrees F. Line a 15-by-10-inch baking pan with parchment paper. Place the salmon in the prepared pan. Whisk vinegar and honey in a small bowl; drizzle half of the mixture over the salmon. Sprinkle with salt and pepper.
- Roast the salmon until the thickest part flakes easily, about 15 minutes. Drizzle with the remaining vinegar mixture.
- Coat a 10-inch nonstick skillet with cooking spray; heat over medium heat. Add bell pepper and jalapeño; cook, stirring frequently, just until tender, 3 to 5 minutes. Remove from heat. Stir in scallion greens.

- Top 4 of the salmon fillets with the pepper mixture and parsley. Serve with pilaf. (Refrigerate the remaining salmon for another use, see Note.)

# MEDITERRANEAN SALAD RECIPES

# GRILLED BANANA PEPPER SALAD

If you don't like hot peppers, make sure to choose sweet banana peppers for this recipe.

Serves 6

- 6 hot banana peppers (AKA Hungarian or wax peppers)
- 1/2 cup Greek feta cheese, crumbled
- 2 tablespoons extra-virgin olive oil
- 2 tablespoons wine vinegar
- 1 teaspoon dried oregano

**Directions**

- Grill peppers until they are soft and their skins are charred, approximately 8–10 minutes; peel.
- Spread peppers flat on a serving dish; add feta over top of peppers.
- Drizzle a little olive oil and some wine vinegar over everything.
- Finish with a sprinkle of oregano, and serve.

# DANDELION GREENS

Serves 6

- 4 pounds dandelion greens
- 1/2 cup extra-virgin olive oil
- 1/2 cup fresh lemon juice Salt and pepper to taste

## Directions

- Cut away and discard stalks of dandelion greens; wash thoroughly.
- Bring a large pot of water to a rolling boil; add greens and stir. Cook over high heat until the greens are tender, about 8–10 minutes; remove and drain well.
- Combine olive oil, lemon juice, salt, and pepper; use as a dressing for the greens. Can be served warm or cold, as a side for grilled fish, or on their own with some crusty bread, kalamata olives, and feta. Garnish with fresh minced garlic.

# Chickpea Salad with Yogurt Dressing

Total time: 30 minutes

Prep time: 30 minutes

Cook time: 0 minutes

Yield: 4 servings

**Ingredients**

**Dressing**

- 1 tbsp. freshly squeezed lemon juice
- 1 cup plain nonfat Greek yogurt
- ¼ tsp. cayenne pepper
- 1½ tsp. curry powder

**Salad**

- 2 15-oz. cans chickpeas, rinsed and drained
- 1 cup diced red apple
- ½ cup diced celery
- ¼ cup chopped walnuts
- ¼ cup thinly sliced green onions
- ⅓ cup raisins
- ½ cup chopped fresh parsley
- 2 lemon wedges

**Directions**

- Make dressing: In a small bowl, whisk together lemon juice, yogurt, cayenne, and curry powder until well combined.
- Make salad: In a large bowl, toss together chickpeas, apple, celery, walnuts, green onions, raisins, and parsley.

- Gently fold in the dressing and season with sea salt and pepper.
- Serve garnished with lemon wedges.

# MEDITERRANEAN POULTRY RECIPES

# SLOW-COOKED DUCK

You'll need a day's head start on this recipe. Slow-cooking makes any ingredient extremely tender.

Serves 6

- 3-pound duck
- 6 bay leaves
- 1 bunch parsley stems, chopped
- 2 tablespoons coarse salt
- 1 teaspoon black pepper
- 1/2 bunch sage 1/2 bunch thyme 1/2 cup olive oil

**Directions**

- Remove and discard all the skin and visible fat from the duck. Cut the duck into serving portions.
- Place the duck in a single layer on a baking sheet. Cover the duck with the herbs and spices. Wrap with plastic wrap. Refrigerate overnight. Rinse and dry thoroughly before baking.
- Preheat the oven to 250°F.
- Place the oil in a baking dish. Add the duck, cover, and bake for 8–12 hours. Allow the duck to cool for approximately 1 hour.
- Thoroughly drain off and discard the oil from the duck; remove bay leaves. Transfer the duck to a broiler pan; flash under the broiler to brown before serving.

# GOOSE BRAISED WITH CITRUS

Serves 6

- 2 yellow onions
- carrot
- stalk celery
- grapefruit
- 2 oranges
- lemon
- lime
- tablespoon olive oil
- 3-pound goose
- 1/2 cup port wine
- 1/4 cup honey 2 cups Hearty Red Wine Brown Stock

**Directions**

- Preheat the oven to 350°F.
- Cut the onions into wedges. Peel and cut the carrot into quarters. Roughly chop the celery. Quarter the grapefruit, oranges, lemon, and lime (leave the peels on).
- Heat the oil to medium-high temperature in a large Dutch oven. Sear the goose on all sides. Add the vegetables and fruit; cook for 5 minutes, stirring constantly. Add the wine and reduce by half, then add the honey and stock. When the liquid begins to boil, cover and braise in the oven for 3–4 hours.
- Serve the cooking liquid (which will thicken as it cooks) as a sauce accompanying the goose.

# SAGE-RICOTTA CHICKEN BREASTS

Serves 6

- 6 chicken breast halves with bone and skin on
- 6 fresh sage leaves
- 1⁄2 cup part-skim ricotta cheese 1 egg white
- 1⁄4 cup niçoise olives Fresh-cracked black pepper, to taste

## Directions

- Preheat the oven to 375°F.
- Rinse the chicken in cold water. Using your finger, make an opening in the skin where the wing was joined and loosen the skin away from the breast. Slice the sage.
- Mix together the sage, cheese, and egg, and place this mixture in a pastry bag. Pipe the mixture under the skin through the opening you made. Place the chicken on a rack in a baking dish; roast for approximately 30– 45 minutes, until the internal temperature of the chicken reaches 165°F and the outside is browned.
- Remove pits and chop olives. After you remove the chicken from the rack, sprinkle with olives and pepper, and serve.

# TURKEY TETRAZZINI

Serves 6

- 1 pound boneless, skinless turkey
- 1 leek (white part only)
- 3 cloves garlic
- 3 cups mushrooms
- 1/4 cup olive oil, divided
- 1/8 cup bread crumbs
- 1/4 cup all-purpose flour
- 1 cup skim milk
- 2 ounces Parmesan, grated
- 2 ounces Romano, grated
- Fresh-cracked black pepper, to taste

**Directions**

- Preheat the oven to 375°F.
- Cut the turkey into bite-size portions. Slice the leek and mince the garlic. Clean the mushrooms with a damp paper towel, then slice them. Mix half of the oil with the bread crumbs.
- Heat the remaining oil over medium heat in a medium-size saucepan; brown the turkey, then remove and keep warm. Add the leeks, garlic, and mushrooms to the pan that you cooked the turkey in; cook thoroughly, then add the flour.
- Whisk in the milk, stirring constantly to avoid lumping. Remove from heat and add the cheeses. Spoon the mixture into a casserole pan and top with bread crumb

mixture; bake for 30 minutes. Season with pepper before serving.

# MEDITERRANEAN SEAFOOD RECIPES

# HALIBUT ROULADE

Serves 6

- 1-pound halibut fillet
- 1/2 pound shrimp 3 limes
- 1/4 bunch cilantro 3 cloves garlic
- 1/2 leek 1 tablespoon olive oil
- Fresh-cracked black pepper, to taste
- 1 cup seafood Demi-Glace Reduction Sauce

## Directions

- Soak 12 wooden skewers in water for at least 2 hours.
- Preheat grill.
- Clean the halibut and keep chilled. Completely remove the shells and tails from the shrimp (save for future use in stock). Slice the shrimp in half lengthwise and remove the veins. Juice 2 of the limes and grate the rinds for zest. Cut the remaining lime into 6 wedges. Reserve 6 whole leaves of cilantro for garnish and chop the rest. Mince the garlic and finely slice the leek.
- Butterfly the halibut fillet lengthwise to make a 1/2- to 3/4-inch-thick fillet. Lay the fillet out, then layer the shrimp, half of the lime zest, half of the chopped cilantro, the garlic, and leek. Gently roll up the stuffed fillet, then cut into 6 pinwheels. Insert 2 skewers into each pinwheel, forming an X, which will hold the pinwheels together. Brush with some of the oil, and grill for 4 minutes on each side.

- To serve, sprinkle each with pepper and the remaining zest and cilantro. Drizzle with the remaining oil and Demi-Glace Reduction Sauce.

# PARCHMENT SALMON

Serves 6

- 1⁄4 cup Compound Butter
- 1⁄2 pound fresh forest mushrooms
- 1 tablespoon minced shallot
- 2 bunches green onions, chopped
- 2 teaspoons chopped fresh marjoram
- 11⁄2 pounds salmon fillet
- 1⁄4 cup dry white wine

## Directions

- Combine the butter, mushrooms, shallot, green onions, and marjoram. Roll in parchment paper and chill for a minimum of 6 hours, until firm.
- Preheat the oven to 400°F.
- Cut the salmon into 4 portions and place each on a folded sheet of parchment paper. Top each with 2 ample slices of the butter. Sprinkle each with about 1 tablespoon of the white wine. Fold up each, folding the parchment over the top and continuing to fold until well sealed.
- Roast for 7–10 minutes, until the paper is slightly brown. Slit open paper and serve immediately.

# BARBECUED MARINATED TUNA

Serves 6

- 1⁄2 pounds fresh tuna
- 1⁄4 cup apple juice
- 1⁄4 cup dry red wine
- 1 tablespoon olive oil
- 1⁄2 tablespoon honey
- 1⁄4 cup minced serrano chili pepper Zest of 1 lemon
- 2 anchovies, chopped
- Fresh-cracked black pepper, to taste

**Directions**

- Rinse the fish in ice water and pat dry.
- Blend together the juice, wine, oil, honey, chili, and zest. Pour the mixture over the tuna and let marinate for 30 minutes.
- Preheat grill.
- Place the fish on the grill (reserve the marinade) and cook for 2–4 minutes on each side, depending on the thickness of the fish and desired doneness.
- While the tuna cooks, place the marinade in a small saucepan over medium heat and reduce by half.
- To serve, plate the tuna and drizzle with marinade syrup, then sprinkle with anchovies and pepper.

# FISH CHILI WITH BEANS

Serves 6

- 1 1/4 pounds fresh fish (sea bass, halibut, or red snapper)
  1 leek
- 1 medium yellow onion
- 12 fresh plum tomatoes
- 4 ounces firm tofu
- 1 fresh jalapeño
- 1 fresh serrano
- 1 teaspoon curry powder
- 1 teaspoon chili powder
- 1/4 teaspoon cayenne pepper Fresh-cracked black pepper, to taste
- 2 tablespoons olive oil
- 2 cups cooked beans (pintos, cannellini, or red kidney)
- 1/2 cup dry red wine
- 1 cup Seafood Stock
- 1/2 cup brewed strong coffee 1 teaspoon brown sugar
- 1 tablespoon honey

## Directions

- Rinse the fish in ice water and pat dry. Slice the leek and medium-dice the onion. Dice the tomatoes. Cut the tofu into large dice. Mince the jalapeño and serrano. Mix together the curry and chili powders, the cayenne, and black pepper.

- Heat most of the oil over medium heat in a large saucepan. Add the leeks, onions, tomatoes, and tofu; cook for 2 minutes. Sprinkle with some of the seasoning mixture, then add all the remaining ingredients except the fish; stew for approximately 60 minutes.
- Preheat grill to medium temperature.
- Brush the fish with the remaining olive oil and seasoning mixture; grill on each side until cooked through (the cooking time will vary depending on the type of fish and thickness), about 5–15 minutes.

To serve, ladle the stew into bowls and top with grilled fish

# MEDITERRANEAN MEAT, BEEF AND PORK RECIPES

# APRICOT-STUFFED PORK TENDERLOIN

Serves 6

- 1½-pound pork tenderloin 1 shallot
- 3 cloves garlic
- 6 apricots
- ½ cup pecans
- 3 fresh sage leaves
- Fresh-cracked black pepper, to taste
- Kosher salt, to taste
- Cooking spray

**Directions**

- Preheat the oven to 375°F.
- Butterfly the tenderloin by making a lengthwise slice down the middle, making certain not to cut completely through.
- Mince the shallot and garlic. Remove pits and slice apricots. Chop the pecans and sage.
- Lay out the tenderloin. Layer all ingredients over the tenderloin and season with pepper and salt. Carefully roll up the loin and tie securely.
- Spray a rack with cooking spray, then place the tenderloin on the rack and roast for 1–1½ hours. Let cool slightly, then slice.

# STEWED SHORT RIBS OF BEEF

Serves 6

- 12 plum tomatoes
- 2 large yellow onions
- 1½ pounds short ribs of beef
- 1 tablespoon ground cumin Fresh-cracked black pepper, to taste
- 1 tablespoon olive oil
- 1 cup dry red wine
- 1 quart Hearty Red Wine Brown Stock

## Directions

- Preheat the oven to 325°F.
- Chop the tomatoes. Roughly chop the onions. Season the ribs with cumin and pepper.
- Heat the oil over medium-high heat in a Dutch oven, and sear the ribs on all sides. Add the onions and sauté for 2 minutes, then add the tomatoes and sauté 1 minute more. Add the wine and let reduce by half.
- Add the stock. When stock begins to boil, cover and place in oven for 1– 1½ hours.
- Drain the ribs and vegetables, reserving the stock. Keep the ribs and vegetables warm. Place the stock on the stove over high heat and let the sauce thicken to a gravy-type consistency.

# SICILIAN STUFFED STEAK

Serves 6

- 1 pound fresh baby spinach
- 5 eggs, divided
- 1 small yellow onion
- 4 cloves garlic
- 1/2 bunch Italian parsley 1/2 cup olive oil, divided
- 1/2 cup grated pecorino Romano cheese 1/4 pound ground veal Kosher salt, to taste
- Fresh-cracked black pepper
- 2-pound round steak
- 1/2 pound prosciutto, diced
- 1/2 pound provolone or Asiago cheese, diced
- 1 cup dry red wine
- 1 cup veal stock
- 2 teaspoons tomato paste

**Directions**

- Place the spinach in a saucepan and gently steam over medium heat until tender, about 8–10 minutes. Remove from heat and let cool. Drain and squeeze out as much water as possible.
- Hard-boil 3 of the eggs, peel, and set aside. Finely dice the onion and mince the garlic. Chop the parsley.
- Heat 1/4 cup of the oil over medium heat in a sauté pan; sauté the onion and garlic until golden. Set aside.
- Preheat the oven to 350°F.

- Mix together the Romano cheese, ground veal, parsley, onion, and garlic. Season with salt and pepper. Add the 2 raw eggs and mix again. Spread the mixture evenly over the round steak. Place the slices of hard-boiled eggs in a row on top of the meat and the cheese mixture. Top with diced prosciutto, provolone, and spinach. Roll the meat tightly over stuffing and tie with string to secure it during cooking.
- Brown the meat in the remaining oil until browned all over. Place in an ovenproof pan. In a saucepan, bring the wine, stock, and tomato paste to a boil. Pour this mixture over the meat and roast in the oven for 1½–2 hours, until the internal temperature reaches 165°F. Turn the meat often to baste.
- Remove the meat from the pan and let stand for about 10 minutes before removing the string. Cut into slices and serve with the remaining juices.

# SAUSAGE PATTIES

Serves 6

- 2 ounces pork fat
- 2 ounces pancetta
- 1/2 pound ground pork
- 1/2 pound ground veal 1 egg
- 1 tablespoon fresh-cracked black pepper, to taste 1 tablespoon dried sage
- 1/4 teaspoon dried red pepper flakes
- 1 teaspoon ground cumin Kosher salt, to taste
- 1 tablespoon olive oil

**Directions**

- Finely dice the pork fat and pancetta. Mix together all the ingredients except the oil until thoroughly blended; form into patties.
- Heat the oil over medium heat in a skillet. Brown the patties on each side, covered with a lid to ensure thorough cooking. Drain on a rack lined with paper towels, then serve.

# VEGETARIAN AND LEGUMES MEDITERRANEAN RECIPES

# RATATOUILLE

Serves 6

- 1 small eggplant
- 1 small zucchini squash
- 1 small yellow squash
- 1/2 leek 1 plum tomato
- 1 shallot
- 2 cloves garlic
- 2 sprigs marjoram
- 1/4 cup kalamata olives
- 1/2 teaspoon olive oil
- 1 cup Basic Vegetable Stock
- Fresh-cracked black pepper, to taste

## Directions

- Large-dice the eggplant, zucchini, yellow squash, leek, and tomato. Finely dice the shallot and garlic. Mince the marjoram and chop the olives.
- Place all the ingredients in a saucepot and cook over low heat for 1 1/2 hours.
- Summer and Winter Squash
- You will often hear yellow squash referred to as "summer squash." Squash is normally divided into two groups: summer squash and winter squash. Summer squashes have thin skins and soft seeds. Winter squashes have tough skins and hard seeds.

# VEGETABLE TERRINE

Serves 6

- 1 medium-size baked sweet potato
- 1 large par-baked baking potato
- 1 medium-size yellow onion
- 3 red bell peppers
- 1 large eggplant
- 4 cloves garlic
- 1 head escarole
- 2 tablespoons olive oil
- 1 tablespoon curry powder
- Fresh-cracked black pepper, to taste
- 1⁄4 cup chopped unsalted cashew nuts

## Directions

- Preheat the oven to 375°F.
- Peel and mash the sweet potato. Peel and slice the baking potato into 1-inch-thick slices. Thickly slice the onion. Cut the peppers in half and remove the seeds. Slice the eggplant lengthwise into 1-inch slices. Mince the garlic. Steam the escarole.
- Brush the onion, peppers, and eggplant with the oil, then sprinkle with curry and black pepper; roast in the oven until al dente, approximately 10–20 minutes.
- Grease a loaf pan with the remaining oil. Line the pan with the eggplant, allowing the slices to drape up and over the sides of the pan. Then layer the remainder of the

ingredients and sprinkle with remaining curry and drizzle with oil. Fold over the eggplant slices to seal the terrine.

- Seal tightly with plastic wrap and place something heavy on top to press the ingredients firmly together. Refrigerate for at least 4 hours.
- Cut into 2-inch slices to serve.

# ZUCCHINI PARMESAN

Serves 6

- 3 medium zucchini
- 2 egg whites
- 1 cup skim milk
- 1/2 cup bread crumbs 1 teaspoon olive oil
- 2 cups Long-Cooking Traditional Tomato Sauce (see recipe in Chapter 2) 6 ounces part-skim mozzarella cheese, shredded
- Fresh-cracked black pepper, to taste

**Directions**

- Preheat the oven to 375°F.
- Slice the zucchini into 1/2-inch-thick coins. Beat the egg whites and mix with the milk. Brush a baking sheet with the oil. Dip the zucchini into the egg mixture, then into the bread crumbs, and shake off excess; place on baking sheet and bake for 10–15 minutes, until the zucchini are just fork-tender.
- Ladle the sauce into a large casserole or baking dish. Cover the bottom of the dish with a single layer of zucchini, then top with the cheese, then sauce. Repeat the process until you have used all the ingredients; bake for 5–10 minutes, until the cheese has melted and begins to brown on top. Top with black pepper, to taste, and serve.

# SQUASH AND GOAT CHEESE NAPOLEON

Serves 6

- 1 medium-size yellow squash
- 1 medium zucchini squash
- 1 tablespoon olive oil
- leek
- 1 cup fresh spinach
- 3 cloves garlic
- 1⁄4 cup pitted, black olives, chopped 2 plum tomatoes
- 1⁄4 cup dry red wine 1⁄2 cup Red Wine Vegetable Stock
- Fresh-cracked black pepper, to taste
- 6 ounces goat cheese, crumbled

**Directions**

- Heat grill to medium-high temperature.
- Slice the squashes lengthwise. Coat a pan with some of the olive oil and grill the squashes for approximately 1–2 minutes on each side until al dente.
- Thinly slice the leek and spinach. Mince the garlic and olives. Dice the tomatoes.
- Heat the remaining oil over medium heat in a large saucepan. Add the leek and garlic; sauté for 2 minutes. Add the spinach; sauté 1 more minute. Add the tomatoes, and sauté for 1 minute. Add the wine and stock, and reduce by half.

63

- To serve, layer the ingredients, starting with squashes, then leek mixture, then pepper, olives, and goat cheese—repeating until you've used all the ingredients.

# MEDITERRANEAN
# DESSERTS

# Grape Delight

Total time: 20 minutes

Prep time: 20 minutes

Cook time: 0 minutes

Refrigerator time: 1 hour

Yield: 8 servings

**Ingredients**

- ¾ kg red seedless grapes, washed and drained
- ¾ kg green seedless grapes, washed and drained
- ¼ cup light cream cheese, softened
- ⅓ cup low-fat Greek yogurt
- 1 tsp. vanilla extract
- 2 tbsp. brown sugar
- ½ cup pecans, chopped
- ¼ cup sugar

**Directions**

- Halve the grapes and set aside.
- Combine the cream cheese, yogurt, sugar and vanilla extract until well mixed.
- Add the grapes into the mixture and pour into a large serving dish
- In a separate dish, combine the brown sugar with the pecans and use this to top the grapes mixture completely.
- Refrigerate for at least an hour, then serve.

# Citrus, Honey and Cinnamon

Total time: 10 minutes

Prep time: 5 minutes

Cook time: 5 minutes

Yield: 4 servings

**Ingredients**

- 4 oranges
- 2 tbsp. orange flower water
- 2 tbsp. raw honey
- 1 cinnamon stick
- 2 ½ tbsp. toasted and sliced walnuts

**Directions**

- Peel the oranges and slice them thinly in round shapes.
- Arrange the oranges on a bowl.
- Meanwhile, in a small, heavy saucepan, combine orange flower water, honey and cinnamon stick.
- Stir gently over low heat until the mixture starts simmering, about 2 minutes.
- Pour the hot liquid on the oranges and let it cool, then top with walnuts.
- Best served when cold.

# Sweet Cherries

Total time: 2 hours, 10 minutes

Cook time: 10 minutes

Refrigerator time: 2 hours

Yield: 4 servings

**Ingredients**

- ½ kg fresh cherries, washed and pitted
- 2 cups of water
- ¾ cup sugar
- 15 peppercorns
- 1 small vanilla bean, split
- 3 strips orange zest
- 3 strips lemon zest

**Directions**

- Set cherries aside.
- Add rest of ingredients to a saucepan and bring to a boil, stirring constantly until all the sugar is dissolved.
- Now, add the cherries and simmer for about 10 minutes until soft but not disintegrated.
- Pour out the foam on the surface and set aside to cool.
- Put in the fridge for about 2 hours.
- Strain the liquid before serving.
- Best enjoyed when served with ice cream.

# Summer Delight

Total time: 2 hours 10 minutes

Prep time: 2 hour 10 minutes

Cook time: 0 minutes

Yield: 3 servings

**Ingredients**

- ⅓ kg peaches, sliced
- 2 tbsp. freshly squeezed lemon juice
- ½ bottle of sweet red wine
- 1 tbsp. brown sugar

**Directions**

- Dip the peach slices in lemon to prevent oxidation.
- Pour the wine in a bowl and add sugar to it, then pour in the peaches together with their juice.
- Cover the bowl and refrigerate for at least 2 hours.
- Serve cold.

# MEDITERRANEAN
# BREAD

# PATATOPITA (POTATO PIE)

Serves 6

- 2½ pounds white potatoes 1 cup finely crumbled Greek feta cheese
- 1 cup finely shredded halloumi cheese
- 1 tablespoon finely chopped fresh mint leaves
- Slight pinch nutmeg
- Salt and pepper to taste
- 4 or 5 eggs, well beaten
- 2 tablespoons extra-virgin olive oil
- 1 cup dried bread crumbs

**Directions**

- Preheat the oven to 350°F.
- Wash and peel the potatoes; cut into small chunks. Boil in plenty of salted water until soft, about 30–40 minutes. Drain and place in a large mixing bowl; mash well and leave to cool slightly a few minutes.
- Add cheeses, mint, nutmeg, salt, pepper, and eggs; incorporate well with potatoes, until entire mix is smooth and creamy.
- Using 1 tablespoon oil, grease the pie baking pan well; spread a little less than half of the bread crumbs evenly across the bottom of the pan. Pour the potato pie mix into the greased pan; spread evenly.
- Evenly distribute the rest of the bread crumbs across the top; spray remaining olive oil on top.

- Bake for 40–45 minutes, or until the top is golden brown. Note: The pie will rise while in the oven and will settle when removed to cool, so don't be surprised by either state. Let stand 1 hour before slicing and serving.

# SPANAKOTYROPITA (SPINACH AND CHEESE PIE)

Yields approximately 20 pieces

- 2 pounds fresh spinach
- 1⁄2 cup fresh dill, finely chopped
- 1⁄2 cup fennel leaves, finely chopped
- 2 large leeks, white part only, thinly sliced
- 2 green onions, diced
- 1⁄2 cup extra-virgin olive oil, divided
- 1 pound Greek feta cheese, crumbled
- 2 eggs, lightly beaten
- Salt and fresh-ground pepper to taste 1 package commercial phyllo

**Directions**

- Preheat the oven to 350°F.
- Wash the spinach well; chop coarsely and set aside to drain well. Wash, drain, chop, and combine dill and fennel in a mixing bowl.
- In a large frying pan, sauté the leeks and diced green onions in 2 tablespoons olive oil until soft; set aside in a mixing bowl 10 minutes to cool. Add dill and fennel, feta, eggs, salt, and pepper; mix thoroughly.
- Spread out the phyllo sheet. Lightly brush the sheet entirely with olive oil; spread a line of cheese and vegetable mix along the length of one edge. Roll lengthwise into a long cigar shape with the filling inside.

Curl each cigar-shaped package into a spiral; place on a lightly greased baking sheet.

- Bake for 45 minutes, until golden brown. Serve hot or cold.

# MEDITERRANEAN RICE AND GRAINS

# Gluten-Free Coconut Granola

## Ingredients

- 3 cups certified gluten-free rolled oats
- ½ cup sweetened shredded coconut
- ¼ teaspoon kosher salt
- 1/3 cup maple syrup
- 1 tablespoon canola oil
- ½ cup sliced almonds
- 1 cup dried cranberries

## Preparation

- Preheat oven to 325°F.
- Line a large sheet pan with parchment paper; set aside.
- Combine gluten free oats, coconut, salt, maple syrup, and canola oil in a large bowl.
- Toss ingredients well and pour out onto a prepared baking sheet.
- Bake, stirring occasionally, until golden brown (15 to 20 minutes).
- Remove from oven to cool.
- Once cool, mix in almonds and dried cranberries.
- Enjoy right away or store in an airtight container for up to 2 weeks.

# MEDITERRANEAN EGG AND RECIPIES

# Mediterranean Feta & Quinoa Egg Muffins

**INGREDIENTS**

- 2 cups baby spinach, finely chopped
- 1/2 cup finely chopped onion*
- 1 cup chopped or sliced tomatoes {cherry or grape tomatoes work well}
- 1/2 cup chopped {pitted} kalamata olives
- 1 tablespoon chopped fresh oregano
- 2 teaspoons high oleic sunflower oil, plus optional extra for greasing muffin tins
- 8 eggs
- 1 cup cooked quinoa*
- 1 cup crumbled feta cheese
- 1/4 teaspoon salt

**INSTRUCTIONS**

- Pre-heat oven to 350 degrees fahrenheit, and prepare 12 silicone muffin holders on a baking sheet, or grease a 12 cup muffin tin with oil and set aside.
- Chop vegetables and heat a skillet to medium. Add vegetable oil and onions and saute for 2 minutes. Add tomatoes and saute for another minute, then add spinach and saute until wilted, about 1 minute. Turn off heat and stir in olives and oregano, and set aside.
- Place eggs in a blender or mixing bowl and blend/mix until well combined. Pour eggs in to a mixing bowl {if using a

blender} then add quinoa, feta cheese, veggie mixture, and salt, and stir until well combined.

- Pour mixture in to silicone cups or greased muffin tins, dividing equally, and bake in oven for 30 minutes, or until eggs have set and muffins are a light golden brown. Allow to cool for 5 minutes before serving, or may be chilled and eaten cold, or re-heated in a microwave the next day.

# MEDITERRANEAN
# BREAKFAST BAKE

# Acorn Squash Bread

### Dry Ingredients

- 1 cup raw, shell-free pumpkin seeds
- 2 cups golden flaxseed meal
- ½ teaspoon ground ginger ¼ teaspoon ground nutmeg 1 teaspoon baking soda
- 1½ teaspoons baking powder
- ½ teaspoon sea salt

### Wet Ingredients

2 cups cooked, seeded acorn squash with skin (from 1½ pounds raw, stem-free, seed-free squash; see note)

½ cup liquid egg whites

1 tablespoon vinegar

### Direction

1. Preheat the oven to 350°F.
2. Cover a 12 × 17-inch baking sheet with Pan Lining Paper, foil side down.
3. Grind pumpkin seeds into a fine meal.
4. In a large bowl, mix together the dry ingredients.
5. Blend wet ingredients thoroughly in blender.
6. Transfer the wet mixture to the bowl of dry ingredients. Mix well and quickly.
7. Scrape the batter onto the prepared baking sheet. Push the mixture to the edges, then level with a spatula. Bake for about 30 minutes or until dry to the touch.

8. Place upside down on a cooling rack. Remove the pan and paper. Let cool.

9. After cooling, cut into desired pieces or use as a prebaked pizza crust. Store in a sealed container in the refrigerator.

# Garlic Onion Bread

## Dry Ingredients

- 2 cups raw, shell-free sunflower seeds
- 2 cups golden flaxseed meal
- 2 tablespoons fresh or dried dill
- 1 teaspoon baking soda
- 1 teaspoon baking powder
- ½ teaspoon sea salt

## Wet Ingredients

- 2 cups chopped yellow onion
- 10 garlic cloves
- 1 cup liquid egg whites
- 2 tablespoons vinegar

## Directions

1. Preheat the oven to 350°F.
2. Cover a 12 × 17-inch baking sheet with Pan Lining Paper, foil side down.
3. Grind sunflower seeds into a fine meal.
4. In a large bowl mix together dry ingredients.
5. Blend wet ingredients thoroughly in blender.
6. Transfer the wet ingredients to the bowl of dry ingredients. Mix quickly and well.
7. Scrape the batter on to the prepared baking sheet. Push the mixture to the edges, then level the thickness with a spatula.
8. Bake for 30 minutes or until dry to the touch.

9.  Place upside down on a cooling rack. Remove the pan and paper. Let cool.

10. After cooling, cut into desired pieces or use as a prebaked pizza crust. Store in a sealed container in the refrigerator.

VERSION 2.

# Ranch Onion Bread

### Dry Ingredients

- ½ cup raw, shell-free sunflower seeds
- 1½ cups flaxseed meal
- 1½ teaspoons fresh or dried parsley
- 1½ teaspoons fresh or dried dill
- 1½ teaspoons garlic powder
- ½ teaspoon baking soda
- ½ teaspoon baking powder
- ½ teaspoon sea salt

### Wet Ingredients

- ½ cup chopped onion
- ½ cup chopped zucchini
- ½ cup chopped carrot ¼ cup sour cream
- ¼ cup liquid egg whites
- 1 tablespoon vinegar

### Directions

1. Preheat the oven to 350°F.
2. Cover a 9 × 13-inch baking sheet with Pan Lining Paper, foil side down.
3. Grind sunflower seeds into a fine meal.
4. In a medium bowl, mix together the dry ingredients.
5. Blend wet ingredients thoroughly in blender.
6. Transfer the wet mixture to the bowl of dry ingredients. Mix well and quickly.

7. Scrape the batter onto the prepared baking sheet. Push the mixture to the edges, then level with a spatula. Bake for about 45 minutes or until dry to the touch.

8. Place upside down on a cooling rack. Remove the pan and paper. Let cool.

9. After cooling, cut into desired pieces or use as a prebaked pizza crust. Store in a sealed container in the refrigerator.

# Lemon Garlic Spinach Bread

## Dry Ingredients

- 1½ cups flaxseed meal
- ½ teaspoon baking soda
- ½ teaspoon baking powder
- ¼ teaspoon sea salt

## Wet Ingredients

- ⅓ cup chopped tomato 5 garlic cloves
- 11 cups fresh baby spinach (5–6 ounces)
- ¼ cup liquid egg whites
- 2 teaspoons lemon zest
- 1½ teaspoons white vinegar

## Directions

1. Preheat the oven to 350°F.
2. Cover a 9 × 13-inch baking sheet with Pan Lining Paper, foil side down.
3. In a medium bowl, mix together the dry ingredients.
4. Blend wet ingredients thoroughly in blender.
5. Transfer the wet mixture to the bowl of dry ingredients. Mix well and quickly.
6. Scrape the batter onto the prepared baking sheet. Push the mixture to the edges, then level with a spatula. Bake for about 60 minutes or until dry to the touch.
7. Place upside down on a cooling rack. Remove the pan and paper. Let cool.

8. After cooling, cut into desired pieces or use as a prebaked pizza crust. Store in a sealed container in the refrigerator.

# MEDITERRANEAN APPETIZERS

# Healthy Mediterranean Dip

Total time: 15 minutes

Prep time: 15 minutes

Cook time: 0 minutes

Yield: 8 servings

**Ingredients**

- 1 can pineapple, drained
- ¼ cup coconut, flaked and toasted
- 16 strawberries
- 8 bunches grapes
- 2 nectarines, thinly sliced
- Choc chip cookies

**Directions**

- Mix pineapple, coconut and yogurt in a bowl.
- Serve in 8 smaller bowls and top with fruit and cookies then cover and refrigerate for 1 hour.
- You are ready to eat!

# Mediterranean Salad Kabobs

Total time: 15 minutes

Prep time: 15 minutes

Cook time: 0 minutes

Yield: 24 servings

**Ingredients**

- ¾ cup low fat plain Greek yogurt
- 2 tsp. fresh oregano, chopped
- 2 tsp. fresh dill weed, chopped
- 2 tsp. raw honey
- 1 small clove garlic, finely chopped
- ¼ tsp. sea salt
- 24 toothpicks
- 24 Kalamata olives, pitted
- 24 small grape tomatoes
- 3 English cucumbers, sliced and halved

**Directions**

Mix yogurt, oregano, dill, honey, garlic and salt in a bowl and set aside. Thread an olive, a tomato, half a slice of cucumber on each toothpick and serve with the dip.

CPSIA information can be obtained
at www.ICGtesting.com
Printed in the USA
BVHW091721180621
609900BV00004B/939